DRIFT AND PULSE

Books by Kathleen Halme:

Every Substance Clothed
Equipoise
Drift and Pulse

DRIFT & PULSE

POEMS BY KATHLEEN HALME

Kathleen Halme

Carnegie Mellon University Press

Pittsburgh 2007

Acknowledgments

Blueline: "Comb"

Denver Quarterly: "Rites, Practices, Spells, and Symbols"
and "The Bungalow Museum"

Georgia State University Review: "Futures Always Find
Their Forms"

Gulf Coast: "What Self"

Massachusetts Review: "The Brain Tells Us What is Real"

National Poetry Review: "Are," "Orb," "Port of Entry,"
and "The Galaxies are Where They Ought to Be"

Ploughshares: "Poppy Sleeping"

Poetry: "The Other Bank of the River"

The Oregonian: "Bulls in Clear-cut"

The South Carolina Review: "That Ocean in Which Dropped
Things Are Bound to Sink"

32 Poems: "Apostrophe à Go-Go"

Zyzzyva: "After Incandescence" and "Viewmaster"

The Long Journey: Pacific Northwest Poets, Oregon State University
Press, 2006: "Comb," "Drift and Pulse," and "What Self"

The publication of this book is supported by a grant from the
Pennsylvania Council on the Arts.

Library of Congress Control Number: 2006922782
ISBN-13: 978-0-88748-463-6
ISBN-10: 0-88748-463-8
Copyright © 2007 by Kathleen Halme
Printed and bound in the United States of America

10 9 8 7 6 5 4 3 2 1

Contents

for Alan

Are

Come closer, fall
into the longitude, the form
and flow of god—
an act, a rite, a ritual
we'll never get used to.

Presence or portent,
don't say we had
precious little warning.
That morning on the ripe island

someone placed an enormous pumpkin
on a pile of broken pallets.
It looked like a chrome aurora,
a giant mandarin. Meanwhile,

on the farm island
bees nudged everything.

Down the dirt road
through the bloated orchard we rode
in helmets lined with foam.

Russian women in kerchiefs laughed,
picking mushrooms in the slash.

A girl in a grey veil ducked into a van.

Out of the corn maze swished
two young couples in satins and velvets
brushing off their garments.

Meanwhile,
the teen goat rubbed his horn buds
on anything alive. Where do we insert ourselves
into this richness, this picture?

At the produce stand the pink farmer
told a fat girl to smile and she would not.
He said she should be ashamed.

The four apples in our hands were fifteen cents less a pound,
he said, if we picked them ourselves. We had not.
He said we could ride out and pick some
if we preferred the lesser price.

A woman squirted honey on the back of her hand
and licked. Come back next year with the baby,
the farmer said, handing her a box.
She bought comb and jars and honey sticks.
Bees nudged everything.

Dusk pushed in, aurous and insistent
as everyone closed in
on the fire
and the pumpkin.

The Other Bank of the River

Because personal poetry is no longer
the dominant mode unless, of course,
you are an Other or can tolerate the overkill
of Persephone spitting out her seed,
I'll be impersonal as dust, the lord
protector of less, as self-indulgent as an egg.

Let's blame it on the brain:
I was going to stay asleep until
I could stand music. Smudge of a day through lace,
nothing moves when we lose delight.
I'd been studying inner forms.

Luckily, while I was voodooed numb
and the sun's yolk hardened
over our home, I hadn't made many promises
I couldn't keep. "People die in bed,"
my mother always said, nozzling her Electrolux
through the pink sack of our sleep.

Forget the cruelty
of April, February had fangs,
incisors of mini-daffs and Daphne,
when you pulled me out of bed
to the pale new park
on the other side of the river,
a reclaimed wetland as subtle
as a roll of paper towels.

Who could trust this cicatrix
of post-industrial land planted
with too many little trees trussed

to poles flapping warning signs:
Do not, do not, do not . . .
I felt slippery, a chalaza in a cup
and held tightly to the double helix of us.

Off the paved path (made from
ground-up sneakers) we spotted
a boy dragging a heap of goose
by its fanned-out wing, the neck flopping
like a question mark. His free hand
struck at a small woman pulling him, who was,
in life, his mother. She had a face
like a mink and was screaming about disease.
The boy yelled to us, "This one's already dead!"
and held the goose like a bagpipe.

What will suffice is pleasure,
every golden egg. Pain fits less
into ellipses. Again, I apologize
for the three-pound storm
that is my brain and me.

Vie

Vie, of course, means life in French, a syllable I like,
but put pressure on the i and you get a fight
for place, for love, for prey.
When it comes to barking back, I hide;
"Have some more," my mother said to Cerberus
as my father filled the dog dish.
Wounded by a lie, wouldn't it be wise to bare one's incisors?
"To a sweet girl, I'm sorry I didn't know you better."
The yearbook scribbles weren't meant to be unkind.
A specimen of my own sincerities and working class,
I'm still unknown and nice, one advantage of being
sessile in the surge. Anemones wince like fists
and barnacles crowd and crush and undercut. Bivalves secrete
more luster than mermaids stringing matinees of pearls.

The Galaxies are Where They Ought to Be

When will you view the realm without obstruction,
luculent and colored-in like photographs of nebulae
the naked eye will never see? Keep rehearsing sanctity.
You bought a house as is. The agent tranced and touched
the beadboard, sniffing old-growth lumber and Victorian bleach
as gauze unwound on porcelain knobs inside the fissured plaster.
He had hands like countries, inviolate and clean; he staged
a self susceptible to you. Weren't you the girl
with aching braids, waiting by the wedding cake
for the server to scrape frosting roses onto your plate?

Three hundred million years ago, when x did equal y,
at least in genes and pairs, your kind swapped codes
like every earthbound animal. Your lot churns artifacts rising
from the load. Big tooth, pink comb, thimble filled with worms,
       the DNA of acts.
Keep cadence with a rake: brain is to mind as house is to home.
Brain/mind, house/home. Galileo's finger is still shriveled in a dome.

To Klickitat and Back

On walks I take to calm my brain,
I've found a black eye patch, a scrapbook
full of postwar baby cards, an eyeglass lens,
a jar of charms, a suede pouch in a bush.
The neighborhood keeps sloughing stuff,
and excess begs attention like putti buzzing
heads of demigods in muggy Florentine
museums. I used to drive between the mounds
on big trash day, loading up wood furniture
as though we were preparing for a rite.
Our footprint isn't big enough to keep collecting
artifacts; it's sad to find your things.

My heart goes out to _____
is an expression I can't stomach in this post-safe age.
I loathe the image of the organ springing
like a meatball of easy emotion; I'd rather die
a hobo of loneliness than have flesh ping-pong
my lawn deer. Shed skin and scale and carapace,
nothing scares me more than you;
I'd give back anything, save me.
As long as it takes, I always say.
My hypothalamus moans for you.
I'll keep you in my godspot
until it doesn't hurt.

Rites, Practices, Spells, and Symbols

§

In that dream life you lead
a well-brushed miniature donkey,
ink sloshing in his saddle casks.
Is it for beauty, is it for balance?
In their olive shade villagers in linen
have been waiting for you,
rinsing empty mouth-blown bottles.

§

Egyptian ink was lampblack stirred with gum
or glue. A writing fluid should bite
into the surface, but it smudged
the scribe's parchment and papyrus.
Death and always death, he cursed,
listening to his brain.

§

For natural ink, you'll need to squeeze the ink bag
of an inkfish, a master of emotion;
you'll find the opening near the anus.
Careful! This fish can squirt
a black cloud to hide itself from hurt.

§

When they were new at this,
it didn't occur to her
to take him inside her.
She wanted to behold
the unbelievable convulsion.

By the waterfall they slotted their skis
in powder and lay in a hollow after
the oldest ink shimmed their drift.

§
Infinite Ink™
see: www.ii.com/math

§
Make your own ink: look for little nut-like bumps
on oaks, where the female gall wasp lays her eggs.
Crush these excrescences in your mortar and pestle,
soak in rain. Strain through linen. Add copperas.
Add gum arabic. Pour into bottles, cork, and label.
Fill your pen.

§
To make a tiny hand
Victorian ladies preferred crow
to goose quills. The five outermost quills pulled
from the left wing of a live goose in spring
were suited to the common right-hand slant.

§
Whole milk written on white bond
was invisible until her girlfriend toasted
the note and words ghosted up their gold:
Come over when my parents leave for bingo—
we can play my father's dirty record.

The 45 sang the secret song about a woman
who slept with a fountain pen. "She gave birth
to a colored child," the record claimed. An uncut deck
of naked lady playing cards fenced our girls in sunsuits,
tied by mothers at their shoulders. Inkhorn, ink sac, and fresh nib.
Ink that is invisible is called sympathetic ink.

§
Have you tasted ink?
I learned about this ritual from an anthropologist
who had seen substantial metaphoric grief: write
your prayers in ink then soak the paper in a glass of water.
Discard the paper and drink.
Surprisingly, to me, it tasted bitter,
considering what it was.

The Sun, The Moon, The Sea, and Men and Women

I.

Walter's fishless koi pond bubbles the bathysphere
of Carmeline's beloved sleep; she leans into the canyons, the drifts.
There would be pears: the gold, the red, the green. She loved

the restoration of the world in miniature. The sea inside
the pond seemed safe, although raccoons had scrapped their feasts,
laying out the dainty skeletons on lily pads,
before they washed their happy hour hands and faces.

On ladders of various lengths, in ponytail and kilt,
Walter miters new window frames for his mossy bungalow.
His hand saw pull-pulls her overprecious sleep.

Undrugged, she is kneeling in the dirt, prying apart
a clump of bulbs that has grown too tight to form
into bearded irises. The fist of corms looks like a kraken.
All year she's been growing a new face,
one that won't scare babies.

Plosive and lovable, Walter the brave has crossed the street
to tell her about some birds that have returned from Mexico.
He rubs a plum cloud onto his overalls
with its hidden rectangular pencil.
In the grass she sees the bubble in his level trying to center.

When will I get used to men, she wonders, sliding
back her headscarf, as Walter says, "you can't imagine how
it looks: two thousand notched wings circling."

II.

Elaborate suppers unfold on quilts around the chimney,
stand-in for the missing old growth snags.
Inside, the birds have constructed a colossal nest
with saliva and twigs, a collapsible yet necessary structure.

The schoolyard is also artful. Someone with patience
has stacked sticks into tiny human shapes and dwellings.
A little teepee and a lean-to with snail shells circled
inside as though it were a place of ritual.

A man throws a braided esophagus
for a his roan dog's pleasure, then the sun falls
over the edge of everything, and the moon thumbs
its brass counterweight in an old-fashioned gesture.

"There's usually more than none," a woman gripes,
folding a red blanket as her girl tosses an apple core.
Look! Two bugs with feelers are already investigating.

The mother and daughter don't seem to know
they are as lovely as cloudberries.
"Mandibles," Carmeline decides.

III.

For this romance I fabricated lies.
Did you expect the truth? Why?
Any core sample of the universe
is fiction on the front and back and sides,
the same story: we sublimed, we died.

That Ocean in Which
Dropped Things are Bound to Sink

Marianne Moore, "A Grave"

The baby gums the bars,
blinking down the panthers

holding up a lampshade—
a thick corporeal spell!

Dark is the blond tv, a diving bell.
The world soaks through.

She is these things
yet she did not create them.

All the baby wants is everything
to come close enough to eat.

Though nothing here is good enough
her first known word is *ma*.

Mother is sleeping off the nightshift
in her ether slip. Winged cap,

a starched bird on the bureau,
seed pearl on her nurse's pin.

The me/not me of breathing
shears the bedroom walls.

That baby in the living room
could cry itself to pieces.

What I Paid For/Things to Do/Be Conscious Of

I want this
to be quick,
I want this
to be brutal.
I want this
to be the opening
you'll never need.
It was a girl I saw

on the front red steps of a pre-rehabbed bungalow,
the kind most of our friends have bought, or want,
built a hundred years ago to be a "permanently satisfying home,"
a girl's hand sliding in and out of a box of Ritz.

Four giants in skins glided up in a Mercury. One rolled back
a quart of steel. Then at the bottom of her steps,
the biggest raised his arms in a molting gesture:
I am the champion, I am a bear,
my arms are not attached to me.

And most remarkable to me,

her face did not float into terror or embarrassment.

It emptied, as though she had the power to bust the stitches
of her fontanelle and squirt a field to hide herself.

On bikes, nerds in helmets, we streamed by.
I used to ride without protection, but twice in my adult life I struck
my head, skin to skull, wide open. It had to be Sunday morning:

the moment was arching with imagination, yet all I witnessed
was her small hand plowing in the box, pink and aqua barrettes
nodding, and through the threshold, a woman inside
splayed like a compass rose.

Sap

You poor whiner, insured to claim
your troubles are unique.
Where were *you*
when the green sponge gave suck?

Pain revives a landscape.

In the pre-feast days of rain,
the looping scenes of wet and rot,
the hammer of a manual is taking down
the day the skid row's old growth
stumps stayed cloaked in moss.

You have seen them stilled
in photographs; not as sad as you,
they belonged to one another,
a family waltzing on a tree stump:
the tincture of selves and circumstance
on a cedar's flat seeping.

There was a boy, a grease monkey,
who bought a bath, an hour of girl.
Afterwards he posed in the notched undercut,
one wet grin before the crosscut.
He was clean the evening of the mowing down.

Meriwether

We don't want our heroes to succeed at suicide;
we're too busy murdering each other. Let's back up

to the miserable expedition, when geography was a neurowish
for mythic symmetry, a mirrored landmass with a Mississippi hinge.

Details suck in sentimentalists: he hauled pewter penis syringes.
In Oregon, fecund and horrible, the Gorgon of rain, he craved salt

and made some with his men, boiling seawater to kill time in rain.
We want him to go home, to stay in love with the possible,

to stop, by will alone, his tumbling into the intolerable logic
of a melancholic brain. We've been duped by the rewrite

of the roughneck inn, robbers shooting him to death,
grabbing money from his saddlebags, leaving the red notebooks

filled with minutiae of lands and tribes, exostars in skies.
When he suicided, no one who knew the man named

like a brightening mood was surprised. He'd already tried.
Witnesses at the inn say he raved and paced, told wild lies, he spread

his bearskins on the floor. He could no longer sleep in a bed,
now he would simplify his mind. Dear reader, should anyone

be forced to live? He shot his forehead with a pistol,
then he shot his chest. He cut in with his razor.

"I am so strong," he said, "it is so hard to die."
Although the news was sad, no one was surprised.

The Bungalow Museum

There is a privacy of mind that can shine
a slight opening in an other.

In the clearing, the field was white,
the sky produced two moons.

We found the blue bungalow
in a grove of sugar pine. Displayed

inside, a walrus hide stretched into a boat,
a seal intestine parka, mukluks

sewed from salmon skin. I'd read about
these artifacts. They made me sadder

than I was. I would finish alone.
Pelt still on the creature

thought of as hide. Gray whale
slipping out her calf in a cloud of duff.

A Diversion

A satellite shot coordinates to their unit on earth,
orbiting above the couple in the cedars.
Love becalmed them,
on the butte and in the leaning meadow,
where a pioneer orchard of apple trees
shifted in long parallels.

No house, no sheds, no barn,
but the apple grove persisted.
If these trees still presented fruit,
it grew too high for anyone to reach.

Had there been sun, the volcanoes would have appeared
as mountains. The man, who often had unusual luck, easily
found ground zero. On his knees he turned down
the blond grass and pulled out the case by its handle.
Someone else had dug that hole to fit the lunchbox.
Now it was Sunday afternoon, 70 degrees, the sixth of June.

Inside were prizes you would tuck into a drawer,
a white guest book and a loaded camera.

They chose a pin of a pig dressed like
a 19th-century gent and left a holy medal of Saint Dymphna,
inscribed the book and took a photo at arm's length,

though the woman never believed
she looked like herself in photographs.
He raised the grass to hide the cache
as though they hadn't been there.
Soon they passed a man hiking with two boys.

A bright unit similar to their own thumped
his narrow chest like a scapular. The men nodded
as strangers in that town will do. The woman sensed
the smaller boy, the one with the blue forelock,
would find the box and it cheered her.
Clearly, she thought, he was one who noticed things.

Voluptuary

Again, I fall for the delicate brothers in vests,
nouveau Victorians as lovely as paper clips, kittenish
twins selling stationery—paper going nowhere—
and fountain pens' nibbed gold beaks inscribed
with family crests. These men have fobs.
I think of daisy chains. A lady, they

would say, is being waited on. I am that
woman; they know I know I would
buy almost anything in the warm store
of a resistant unconscious: His and His,
ink waves screwed in squat blue bottles,
Venus Velvets boxed in musth. Dears,

they still carry packets of stars, gummed foil
a teacher licks. Their screen is smudged with human oil.
Across the varnished countertop two forms nod
to set theory's overlap. I crave a centered preciousness.
One brother soft slides towards me—
sounds like velvet slippering mahogany—

a packet of deckle-edged cream, laid paper
embossed last month in Paris: a vellum hand
with cabochon pressed the curve of two discrete
gold dolphins, parallel apostrophes
swimming a billet-doux to my brain.
"I hope this is what you'll need."

Port of Entry

Wary of the counterfeit emotion
jangling at the oyster bar,
the saxophonist in oilskin
rested on a saltplank, a man
and his alto sax alone
on the outer harbor.

Although he seemed
transparent, he was occupied
with a terrible disorder,
the pawl of everything
that spun his orbit.

love apple
lovebird
love feast
love knot
love-lies-bleeding

Had you observed him,
you would have noticed
his preoccupation
with the man-of-war
floating below him in the inky harbor,
roaming like a clear blue land

unmoored aboard its roots.
He studied it like permanence,
a pellucid delicious.
Sometimes he could tongue his thoughts
in reedy elegance.

The organism was about
to touch a cabin cruiser,
a pleasure boat of gloss and trim,
odd among the market boats
in the brothy harbor.

Who had he been, this stranger?
He would slip
below the pellicle,
velvet slots holding
the parts in place
in the oily harbor.

The Maggot in the Mushroom

Mrs. Livingstone shimmied out
of her starchy apron before she would
step outside to give us directions to the tower
where, the guidebook said, miniature
deer ran freely on the grounds. We had
slept fitfully in her grown son's bed,
a rubbery room with dusty planes.
His shaving soap was cracked.
Mrs. Livingstone
had spent her summer raising a litter
of pups, she said, and so her garden
had gone wild. She was dusting
ivory cups as we came down
to breakfast. Turning eggs, she was
polite. There was no telling who
she was or how she liked her sex.

Futures Always Find Their Forms

"Be fun," said the man, pulling
on the ribbon. Was he turning un-nice?
All his junk shifted upstairs.

Drift net, seine net, trap and weir,
fishing wheel and barricade.

"I just hate having something
in my shoe," the woman on the escalator
confided to her daughter.

Who couldn't love a whelk's
folding in and out of form—
yesterday backed to the day before.

Drift net, seine net, trap and weir,
fishing wheel and barricade.

The ceiling/wall split is not major
home repair. Every house shifts.
Little miracle, fill us to July.

They thought they saw a bobbing in the swell.
She waded out to the egg, big as a baby's head.
He placed it in his lettuce garden.

Drift net, seine net, trap and weir,
fishing wheel and barricade.

The Brain Tells Us What is Real

The nuptials were so sweet. The papier-mâché swan
piñata lost its copper beak. Lila took home the head
and S of neck. When the blindfolded bride split the bird

little picture magnets of groom and bride fell
below the cherry tree into the luffing blossoms.
Like quotation marks, a small black baby llama

sprang across the orchard to its mother being petted
over a split rail fence by the wedding party. The cake
was a whipped cream, lemon curd dream. Baskets

of chocolate bars wrapped in their gold names were passed;
we could have kept nibbling the couple into bliss,
but the evening chill was coming in. Hipsters in black

blanched and shifted hips; they held their flutes
then looked relieved when the back-tossed bouquet
of saucer orchids fell at little Rosie's feet. Her sister

has the head and neck; she has the flowers.
The bride and groom are in Hawaii now—asleep—
bubbles breaking across their backs.

Bulls in Clearcut

Above the estuary's eel grass bioelegance,
the bulls stare back,
as shy as lamps.
All thick in winter fur and forelocks, dumb
glamour stock lumbering
through slash.
Their horns jut sideways, forming afterthoughts.
In real woods these bulls
would get racked,
stuck bawling and pumping between fir
and cedar, impossible to turn
heads askance
to pass sidearms through
the understory.

Orb

Don't mind those horses
eating at their altar of alfalfa,
the crabby man in his crushed truck
hauling a load of miniature pumpkins,

salmon pushing like mercury below
the unearthly pink Nooksack casino
double dealed into longhouse,
loghouse, mobile home.

The mind wants more
than an urgency of images, words
furred and folded up like bats
hanging starched and knee-locked in the ward.

Bit by bit, the final form unwinds,
not unlike the bird of paradise
in paradise.

Ooze to ootid, oolite to oolong,
the mind mourns the story
of the central speck
to jell the liquid pearl,
a convenient fantasy of form.

Blame it on the brain,
built mystical to storm the line
of I/not I without the least
belief in gods or signs.

Scape

Erase the
retreat to
the drinkable
lake, the
deer that
preened each
other's backs,
especially Lucky
Devil; delete
the full
cold moon;
cut macho
stellar jays
shrieking in
their cop
suits; delete
the keeper
of the
geese, fumbling
his jumbo
hoop of
keys; backspace
wet man,
wet sky,
wet keys;
delete the
full cold
moon; cut
the cotton
bed, the
mermaid of
the lake,

a violet
dark and
beaded web;
erase the
secret waterfall
and map,
the double
locked canoe
and fire
logs, a
purple cap;
save the
minnows pulsing
wrists; delete
the full
cold moon.

Core

The cave was clean and had an end.

By clanky lantern we saw no artifacts.
No crickets, no crystals, no drippings.
A fireball had cored that hole.
What light there is you bring.

A band of us walked in.
Some glanced back to verify an opening.

The lava tube we penetrated.
The lava tube surrounded us.
"No, one, no, one," murmured the membrane of the cave.

Cushioned with ourselves, magma and mandible,
we were pulled upslope inside the rupture:
the man with a shunt, the woman in her wings,
shivery kids pulling back into daylight.
At the rock fall everyone had to turn back,
blinking off the post-volcanic chill.

I would go back inside if only to see the faces,
faces floating into form, laved and gentled,
intuitive visages, as though we were the only ones
with faces, contrite with forces.

Viewmaster

A common means of access
allowed you go inside.
The sculpted slant was burnished
and swam from eye to eye.
The heavy lid was lifted
and led to lacquered things:
a puffin dipped in godglass
and porcelain apple core.
When seeing swims in seeing
is endlessness restored.

Poppy Sleeping

Lemon light, curd of worry. My eye is all iris.
Look through this small viewer to penetrate
the black shaft. Who's this? Who's that? Green goes
to yellow over there. The eye wants to be investigated
privately. I've lost my sense of humor, vitreous jelly,

a small island floating under a dark mood;
the eye takes shape and raises a bluish moon stuffed
like an olive. Do you see its black center tilting
toward the earth, the honeybees in their filament
harnesses with four wings to organize? The notion
runs to brushy green, a green of aches and quells;
white foams a halo around the poke of red.

Satiny planet penning all shapes separately;
no people, artifacts or habitations on this orbit.
We're silly with light. We need our space.
The brain pulls us to troughs, caldera and chatter mark.
Jump the fence, stick hoof and muzzle into a complicated plot.
Blue thumbprint, green linen, black sash, red dot
licked in its own atmosphere. Hold my place.

What Self

Nothing lived on land, nothing had
crawled out of the shallow sea.

Because they have no hard parts,
it's rare to find the fossil of a jelly.
The farm boy digging a new duck pond
exposed thousands, like old verbs
stranded on the shore of the lonely
Paleozoic; nothing came to eat them,

nothing was sloshing in the shrimpdom.
A see-through diving bell as formal as a ghost,
the giant medusa waved her oral arms to subtilize her food.
Who said life unfolds in language?

Nothing lived on land, nothing had
crawled out of the shallow sea.

Box Jelly

A dream, though real, without a brain will sleep
below the waves from afternoon to dawn.
So muscular it keeps its shape on land,
the Cubozoan bell swings galaxies
of eyes. A neural net is hardly like
our brains, and yet the box retreats from red;
a bag of stunning news more toxic than
a lie. A dream, though real, like consciousness,
flings shooting stars as venomous harpoons,
and one expanding universe implodes.

Drift and Pulse

for Aurelia Labiata, Moon Jelly

Her moon   opens
to   your moon
a pumping   shadow
of heart   no heart
a haloform   an oblate I
underfrilled
in crinolines   a ballgown's
sway   and slave
in champagne stockings
Out of her
element   she is
an apostasy   on paper
eggwhite smear
in a library   book
pulsing iambs   oral arms
fleshpot shadow   of heart   no heart
see   through soul
in plexiglass   No brain   no bones
no spine   no heart
form's form

Apostrophe à Go-Go

O, pardon me, I'm bored
with the nouveau O lassoing
poems as though they were bars
of soap as big as selves

in cellophane. Clean soap
pressed into staying shapes
minus pessimism's
whited sepulchre and itch.

Urgent little swallow, fly
your olive branch
into design . . . elide
in bubbles foaming down:

pulchritude to pretty,
form to form. o driver, o
fulcrum, o splice, o pliers.
See the lower case turn

into a washer? The O proclaims
we still crave halos.

After Incandescence

After we had chased down
every Other, looped the moment's
skein around our wrists,
snuffed a thousand stars from the word

sidereal, traced our birth to words, autopsied
pleasures' pulsing, unpacked the moment's offal,
reconnoitered empty center, turned away
from skidding meanings, fluffed cockalorum's

unfolded form, emptied the beribboned cartons,
eternalized the seconds, examined
all the edges, scraped and scratched
the cuttle bone of consciousness,

worried gaps between our selves,
our words, and stuff, unclothed
every opening, crowned the bits,
scorched the pleats of names and things hissing

their insistence, mourned the crumbling
of the orders, fought the suck of closure,
the tightened knurl of meaning, tossed
the tussie mussie of our power,

I willed myself to god.

Comb

Perhaps I was naïve. I thought it was for beauty:
the bees' stacking their bits of wax
in vertical combs as lattices of six.
The Honeycomb Conjecture now holds this shape
is the most economical partition of a plane
into equal areas and uses the least wax to form
built-ins—the honey, pollen, larvae bins. We know that
bees have three tasks: food, dwelling, toil;
and the food is not the same as the wax,
nor the honey, nor the dwelling.

Did you know you can train honeybees
to come to cardboard flowers?
After you cut out the flower shape you must
place a bottle cap of sugar water in the flower's center.
Pulled to hive, syrup-loaded,
bees tell bees how to find the flowers.

On my desk I keep a cake of beeswax, palm-size
polygon, six-sided, impressed with tiny hexagons,
a six-legged bee raised in the center,
wings folded like a membrane cloaked
in spice of midday beam through leaf.

I smell it every day for faith.
I bought it from a drowsy farm boy yawning
over a glass suitcase of bees working
on their comb. I, too, am an artificer and felt close.
Pure beeswax, it says,
(go in fear of quasivatic drones).

Form of form of form. Sure, it's pure—
wax, wholly wax, yet it mimics maker
and made. It leaves no space.
What if butter came shaped as an udder?
Clumsy jilter of maker and made,
it leaves no space.

I've tried to make way for myth,
but this longing for shapes
as elegant as instinct persists.

Holocene

Opal float, cobalt ocean.
Tell them I AM sent me.

Show me anywhere but in.

My limbic system is convinced
that god's a mystic fit,
built-in like iambs
tocking in our wrists.

A brain knows what it needs.
I pray I am myself,
a non-religious prayer.

And so we dream of bees
and what is not ourselves.

Do you read me?
All in all, I'm yours.

Notes

The factual information about ink-making in "Rites, Practices, Spells, and Symbols" is from **Pen, Ink, and Evidence** by Joe Nickell.

The title "The Sun, The Moon, The Sea, and Men and Women" is appropriated from Keats's letter to Richard Woodhouse, October 21, 1818: "A poet is the most unpoetical of any thing in existence; because he has no identity—he is continually in for— and filling some other Body—The Sun, the Moon, the Sea, and Men and Women . . ."

The title "That Ocean in Which Dropped Things are Bound to Sink" is a line from Marianne Moore's poem "A Grave."

The quotation "a permanently satisfying home" in "What I Paid for/Things to Do/Be Conscious Of" is by Gustav Stickley in his essay, "The Craftsman Idea."

The phrase "earthbound animal" in line 13 of "The Galaxies Are Where They Ought To Be" is borrowed from Dante's *The Divine Comedy*, Canto XIX, line 85: "O earthbound animals! minds as gross as wood!"

In "Comb," the lines "and the food is not the same as the wax, / nor the honey, nor the dwelling" are from Marcus Terentius Varro, *On Agriculture*, III, XVI.